Borrowed Days

Other Books by Marc Plourde

Touchings
(poems, 1970)

The White Magnet
(poems, fiction, one-act play, 1973)

The Spark Plug Thief
(stories, 1976)

Translations

Victor-Lévy Beaulieu: *The Grandfathers* (1975)

Gaston Miron: *The Agonized Life*
(selected poems, 1980)

Juan Garcia: *The Alchemy of the Body and other poems* (1983)

Gaston Miron: *Embers and Earth*
(selected poems, with D. G. Jones, 1984)

Gilbert Langevin: *Body of Night*
(selected poems, 1987)

BORROWED DAYS
POEMS NEW AND SELECTED

MARC PLOURDE

Cormorant Books

Copyright © 2016 Marc Plourde
This edition copyright © 2016 Cormorant Books Inc.

No part of this publication may be reproduced, stored in a retrieval system or transmitted, in any form or by any means, without the prior written consent of the publisher or a licence from The Canadian Copyright Licensing Agency (Access Copyright). For an Access Copyright licence, visit www.accesscopyright.ca or call toll free 1.800.893.5777.

 Canada Council for the Arts   Conseil des Arts du Canada    ONTARIO ARTS COUNCIL CONSEIL DES ARTS DE L'ONTARIO an Ontario government agency un organisme du gouvernement de l'Ontario

Canadian Heritage   Patrimoine canadien

The publisher gratefully acknowledges the support of the Canada Council for the Arts and the Ontario Arts Council for its publishing program. We acknowledge the financial support of the Government of Canada through the Canada Book Fund (CBF) for our publishing activities, and the Government of Ontario through the Ontario Media Development Corporation, an agency of the Ontario Ministry of Culture, and the Ontario Book Publishing Tax Credit Program.

LIBRARY AND ARCHIVES CANADA CATALOGUING IN PUBLICATION

Plourde, Marc, 1951–
[Poems. Selections]
Borrowed days: new and selected poems / Marc Plourde.

ISBN 978-1-77086-468-9 (paperback)

I. Title. II. Title: Poems. Selections.

PS8581.L6A6 2016   C811'.54   C2015-907531-9

Cover art and design: angeljohnguerra.com
Interior text design: Tannice Goddard
Printer: Sunville Printco

Printed and bound in Canada.

CORMORANT BOOKS INC.
10 ST. MARY STREET, SUITE 615, TORONTO, ONTARIO, M4Y 1P9
www.cormorantbooks.com

To the memory of my parents,

Constance Lacombe and Rosaire Plourde,

and to Theresa Krug, with love.

Contents

Where I Began: *Selected Poems*

Gardening at the Dead End of Howard Street	3
In Park Extension	4
On Shannon Street	6
Cousin Jerome	7
Sparrows	8
Branches	9
Some Time Spent on Rachel Street	11
For Monnie	12
Balance: A Railroad Poem	14
Staircase	15
Elizabeth through Winter	16
First Contact	17
Touchings	18
The Couple across the Lane	19
The Hollow	20
In the Park an Old Woman Finds a Bench	21
The White Magnet	22
In an Old Woman's Homeland	24
Three Days' Rain	25
The Tractor	26

The Past Is a Place: *New Poems*

Burning Days, Luminous Sky	29
The Old Streetcar Terminus, Parc Jean Cabot	30
The Pumpkin Field	31
On Salisbury Beach	32
Caesar's Campaigns in Gaul	34
Rooms to Let in Bohemia	36
The Afterlife	38
Tabagie Arsenault, 1920–1972	40
Borrowed Days on Ste-Famille Street	41

The Jacques Cartier Monument in Parc St-Henri	43
Carolyn's Pillbox Hat	45
A Cowhide Mitten Made in China	46
Coming Home to a Flat Where a Light Is Left On	48
On the Winter Steps	50
A Late Night Walk	51
The Dalai Lama at St. Joseph's Oratory	52
Six Months After	54
A Soldier's End on de L'Epée Street	55
The Art of Departure	56
A Prelude	58
Borrowed Minutes, Dying in Hospital	60
The Sea beyond the Coast of Maine	63
Clover, Buckwheat, Wildflower Honey	67
The Shoes of Budapest	69
Life Jacket Drill on a Ship Off San Juan	70
In the Hills of St. Lucia	72
Stray Dogs of St. Lucia	73
Late Recognition	75
A Fall	77
Gospel Music in Little Burgundy	78
Greyhound to Burlington	79
The Unitarian Churchyard in Burlington	80
Notes	83
Acknowledgements	85

WHERE I BEGAN

Selected Poems

Gardening at the Dead End of Howard Street

Lifeless this earth breeds only broken
pieces of glass, tin cans, dust
across its surface

but the man comes anyway; he's an immigrant,
Greek or Italian, and dressed
in torn flannel pants,
checkered shirt and boots

he has come to build a garden.
Determined, his work defies the land,
progresses all day, slow, as

he gathers scrap wood for stakes, pounds
them in with a rock, rakes the dry soil
finally heaps the rubbish
in a pile and sets a flame to it, and rests.

In Park Extension

Some kids never go home. Evenings
they're out front of the poolroom, nervous
to get away, too young still
for a motorcycle
they stand-sit on the curb
seems almost
they grow out of the pavement, are always there
like the cops, the butcher shop, the Greek
pastry store, and old European
toadlike women each day crossing the railroad
to the factory
and back again, they come
bodies toddling
with the weight of their shopping bags full.

April and how this weather is
too cold still, tonight Carol, Dominic, Lagetti
will go looking for an apartment
hallway, one they've not been
kicked out of; half the fun the kids say
is waiting for the janitor
and running.
Carol runs-walks back bent, feet pointed
inward, so is nicknamed "pigeon toes".
It was glue sniffing hurt her
legs, her joints,
she told me
and I didn't believe her at first;
first time I saw her walk I thought it a joke.

Dominic is part of The Tribe,
the neighbourhood gang; he has a red devil's
head etched
on the back of his jacket
and black gloves he flexes his hands in
and makes "snap" leather sounds with,
one fist
hitting the other opened hand, and he has
motorcycle boots, though no motorcycle.
Carol's also part of it;
her initiation came, she says, last week
at the Saint Anthony's
church basement Friday night dance,
in the toilet, they raped her she says.

Music reaches down Howard Street.
Outside, there are kids leaning on a railing,
lighting matches; the jukebox
song comes to them
in pieces, in the traffic
of people opening-shutting the poolroom
door, and it seems
almost they're dancing: Carol, with Lagetti
bent over her, his arms
moving inside her coat. When she turns away
she is tugging her jeans back
up her hips, she laughs and
swears; the popcorn box tucked in her belt
has spilled, pink kernels covering the sidewalk.

On Shannon Street

The house where I began living
was made of old wood
and dust filled with human sound

it was in a district to avoid
walking through because of bums
and derelicts

and the poor always too visible
on galleries and doorsteps
in front of dime stores
cluttering the streets

old men who loafed in the sun
and women in cotton dresses
yelling after their children
down the alley

there I made my first friends
and we climbed over wire fences
into our neighbours' gardens
who'd kick the shit out of us
for stealing

my parents hated that place
and were quick
to move to a better street
where after some time we denied
having lived anywhere else

Cousin Jerome

Cousin Jerome at twelve
was still impenetrable: colours, numbers,
names of streets and so forth, he forgot
always did forget
though his mother kept drilling
"What colour the fridge Jerry, the table, the dress?"

In my mother's kitchen, in front of strangers
he was being humiliated and knew it
though not much more. "Jerry, why'd you flunk
school again?" Pneumonia, they said at the orphanage
after he'd been adopted,
affected him for life.

At seven his brother could already outwit him
and answered questions
in his place, laughing, "Jerry's retarded!"
while Jerome fondled a shirt button or the edge
of the tablecloth; his eyes
were small fish behind glass, turning away.

Sometimes it stopped, talk was directed elsewhere
than Jerome sometimes; at moments
it was silent almost, with water in the kettle boiling
and atop the refrigerator was a yellow wire cage
shape of a beehive, we kept birds in — bird
sound, and my cousin repeating "Don't know, don't."

Sparrows

When I came, the nest was already built.
It is like some large crab hugging the cabin's ceiling.
It is the first thing I see every morning
    after they wake me.
The large one, the mother I think, now perches outside
on the open door and pecks wood.
I've lived here almost one week
and still she considers me an intruder.
Each time she enters, she startles in mid flight
undecided whether to continue to the nest or leave.
At the top of the nest
are four bald heads bobbing in and out, each mouth
a gap red as nail polish. They sing for food.
The singing they make is something I remember of a park
    I knew once,
or what I dreamt of that place before waking: the sound
of swings balancing themselves back and forth
moments after they'd been left.
There was also the old park keeper in a white hat
and some children following him to the gate.

Branches

for Marc and Renée Vanasse

At the start of May
the grounds in certain places were still spotted
with snow not yet melted, despite all the rain
and the small road beside the orchard
could not be walked to its end
and we waited.
When stronger sun came
the apple trees were pruned: cut branches fell
everywhere on the ground, into the mud.
My work was to gather them.
I was told they should be heaped into straight rows
crossing the orchard down the slope; a machine
would come push them away. It took nearly three days
to do this work; it paid for my keep.
After, I shoveled manure from the stables.
They told me I could do nothing else
having come from the city
and not smart enough, unable to repair fences
or help on the tractor, slow at my task and it seemed
even in the smallest things I failed: I cut my hands
and wrists handling the branches,
the rows I made were not always straight.

A girl also worked in the orchard.
She brought me water once in a wine bottle
and her older brother
told me a story he remembered only parts of
from a book; it was
of an old woman some soldiers shot
by mistake: she failed to answer their challenge,
she was deaf. This happened
not far from the orchard he said, in the last century,

and once we visited the monument that was set
at the roadside, a plaque
with her name almost hidden in the grass.

May now has nearly ended.
I live in the city again; I waste time
while the Greek boy who lives upstairs
is climbing a pole
to repair his mother's clothesline, and one leg
brushes against the branches of a small apple tree,
half its blossoms already fallen.

Some Time Spent on Rachel Street

Mornings it woke me: the heat
    itself wakening upon walls, colourless;
    the woman who lived downstairs then was outside
    on her gallery, always

there — fat woman in a black sequined dress, wore no shoes
    and behind her face smudged blue-green with
    makeup, nothing human showed; one stocking was
    half pulled down, if I remember.

Such mornings sickness smell hugged the air, plaster
    and sticky bedclothes. Often, waking I thought
    pleasant thoughts, deliberately.
    Downstairs she sat

detached, dumb, her mind like a worm coiling, burnt
    to the core. As blind, she stared full days
    across the street at nothing, and once
    I felt her looking

at me and wanted to run. One morning
    I slept on a roof, woke surprised at how
    quick the pigeons startled, fled. Children below
    me: one girl looked up; the birds then

were brown hailstones entering clouds.

For Monnie

I can't find her eyes
they move away
then back again

now she's imitating animals
and insects
and bends over the table
squealing in someone's ear

her friends laugh
but just out of politeness,
they don't like her stupid jokes

she's embarrassing
even dangerous
what if the cops
come into this coffee shop

we'll get busted
because of her
an eighteen-year-old

who's been taking drugs:
pot, speed, hash, acid
she mixes them together

too bad for us all
that she had a kid
three months ago
and it's in some orphanage

as it is I don't think
she'll last three more months
everyone in the place is nervous
and looking around

at the other end of the table
Monnie goes on giggling
and making wild faces

Balance: A Railroad Poem

Days now, I spend by the tracks
bent over sitting on broken crates
or in the gravel: quiet

inside, thoughts gather
thin almost as a webbing
of dust they balance

upon the breathing of sounds
through the heat

from all surroundings has come
this grinding of birds,

machines, voices; it hovers
above the railroad, rising
and falling

its sounds entwined
like some thick cloud
of flies, slow heavy insects

that toss and melt upon each other
in the sun

only when a train passes
does the cloud fall, lost

like knotted string in a noise
trembling the earth as it moves
to black hills

of stone on the horizon,
in its echo the insects return —
I listen, tangled with sound

Staircase

As if the sun imprinted itself
along this staircase
I am drawn upward

so small are the grains of light
that they rise from snow
and into my eyes
creating a blankness behind them

I think of nothing, only

that as I move noises move with me:
the crushing of footsteps, strange
wind filled with voices
from opened windows

I have an orange
inside my pocket, its warmth
moving between my fingers

in my room I will peel it

and throw the pieces of skin below,
they will fall like coins
to the sun-glittering steps

small people will look up
and see me, I will laugh
and they will laugh, their faces
so much like pebbles

gathered on the white staircase

Elizabeth through Winter

Fitting, the earth turned a cake of stone
when you died, and how they drilled,
picked, chopped through ice and rock-ground
to find some small black opening and
drop your bones there through the mouth
of winter, and forget you. For pride

I suppose, for fifteen years, Elizabeth,
grandmother, hard from living you lived
alone; unforgiving you refused
fought each of your children's marriages

knowing all along how they'd leave you
to rot. Was it pride made you a charwoman,
grumbling old hag. It would be said you became
the people you came of: farmers, labourers, oxes
in their work, and you could not escape.

A sixty watt lamp's light jets yellow
through the worn shade. Photos before me, faces,
your face lies now in the crust
of this winter sun. The lamp, yours once,

chipped sunflowers crowd its base; now is my heritage
it comes of a past, a time I had no part making
though I will believe and believe the white lace
collar that trims your neck, and here a hair lock
falling near to your eye: eighteen, unmarried, a girl
only, here you are smiling that way I never saw.

First Contact

Several times
her fingers pass over
then settle gently

along the white cup
as if a butterfly
resting on eggshell

that might suddenly break
letting warm coffee
down her dress

Touchings

Seeking roots, your fingertips gather
like white moths onto my eyelids, frail
edges of wings rub lightly back and
forth, soon we are linked
into this touching as though it grew
there, separate from both of us

somewhere below me I have gathered
your face between my palms, my fingers
slowly cross your lips; in their journey
they have stolen your breathing:
warm, moist, I keep it
locked inside my hand

with eyes closed now, only the touching
of your mouth tells me
where I am: it is slow wind moving
down my body and wetness
like the air after it rains, clouds and
trees are turning upon each other

your arms reach to the tallest
branches and they bend
their shoulders to you; my fingers are
now twigs that fall stiff, broken, onto
your breasts, unraveling from them and
from your hair each delicate flower

The Couple across the Lane

Bundled up or not, they find no comfort on the balcony
past October. The old couple have gone in.
For months in warm weather we sat watching each other,
never passing a remark except once
I was throwing crusts on the shed roof below
when the old lady rose frantically waving her arms,
shooing the pigeons:
"They don't give the little fellows a chance!" she said,
meaning the sparrows.
"They certainly don't," I replied.
That sentiment, her indignation, I loved then,
but said nothing.
They gossiped and fought all summer on the balcony.
By August I thought I knew everything,
even the old man's operation, his costly meds,
his angry screams the afternoon she touched his side —
everyone in the lane could hear.
Now they've not been out in weeks,
but today I saw her face alone behind the screen door;
she was looking down at something, at her hands
I guessed then,
resting like stones on her apron.

The Hollow

A storm woke us this morning:
first, thunder — then a downpour
grey and toneless droned on in the dark
while pigeons unmoved by the weather
huddled on the balcony
and lightning appeared like neon in a charcoal sky.
Now, in the kitchen window, I count the flashes,
wait out the seconds between each gleaming fork
and the drawn-out noise —
distant crack of splintering sky —
as if these fragments of time were special, a hollow
in a shell, thunder breaking the shell.

Here in the silence before the crash,
in seconds I can count,
I remember botched intentions,
thoughts of *If I'd done this* and *if* and *if*
that multiply like flashes beyond count,
while in a room down the hall
a woman shuts the alarm before it rings,
turns to the wall and falls asleep and forgets
the day black as night slipping past.

If I could speak — but our talk comes to nothing,
for days we do not speak. We go on,
certain this must be close to the end,
a time between flash and noise,
and neither caring much. If I could squeeze
myself into a ball and sleep —
but this morning I note instead
how the line sways, sags low against the railing,
our clothes are so filled with rain.

In the Park an Old Woman Finds a Bench

In the park an old woman finds a bench
and waits for her breath:
"My breath is gone," she thinks, "it's the heat"
and the heat glistens on her face
and rises with the cut-grass smell of the lawn
now the old woman, who is almost blind,
looks down between her square-toed shoes;
she can feel the stones
with her cane — white glaring stones
"I wish it were shady here," she thinks,
"Oh, it's hot today!"
and the sun is a red splinter in her chest
she swallows
and it picks a hole there, "It's the sun,"
she thinks, on the warm bench
seeing nothing but glare
white points like prongs on a fork
white stones she can feel them
while the sun has picked her insides
now she is an insect shell held
transparent and sightless
on the sun's breath — "My breath," she thinks

The White Magnet

No other movement or sound in this country — one spot
    soft blue-brown
insect in a sugar bowl
I am walking, the whiteness all about me.

Everywhere winter's clean perfect burn,
    the pure ash
curved over belly and heart
of this land I step across, leaves nothing.

No other thought, away from the cold, my head
    floats between
its hands
like a fine vase; fingers tighten round,
knot hard inside my forehead, I may break soon.

Clouded tap-water sky tilted against the snow blade.
    The snow field,
endless
under this sky, is a mirror running;
the absence it gives pinpoints and dazes me.

Before when I stopped, myself breathing was as horses
    breathe and cough
heavy
as a truck motor. Sweat
sapped and ran from my shoulders
and froze. My legs then were stakes, sinking.

Fat flesh of horses heats the stables. I warmed
    my hands once
moving
them slow, over, as if moulding
their flanks. Calves numb almost, my own warmth
now is drained down to the earth. Snow moulds my feet.

The clear frozen distance is an animal; it shreds
    the skin, cuts,
swallows
the insect from its shell.
No other tracks here than my own, I move on,
clumsy as the man who falls, sinks into his shadow.

In an Old Woman's Homeland

This land she once came of, now given
up into evening it resembles
the old woman's death. A thin

wax skin, darkness touches down, rubs its face black
against the road, chokes itself. I am foreign
here. An hour ago, late afternoon,

I think how warm, relaxed, sleeplike it was
where I walked between rainfalls, across the train yard;
green weed smells and oil smells glued to my head,
pulling it, a helium balloon, down. Raining

again. In night this land is also an old woman —
moves past me drawing a silence after her
that winds through the town, the bridge,
its iron arms. Somewhere her reflection drops

on the water and is left there and there is
only absence then. What was it I wanted?
I forget. There was a girl at the roadside,

her face delicate as engraved on a ring,
a blue umbrella turned and turned, flowers opened
with mouths of small cats. All gone now and

the old woman is dead; wax smell rises
from her skin, is some soft white hook hung
in my throat. It rains still. This
doorway I wait in leads to an empty house.

Three Days' Rain

Three days of it, and for two days
it seems I've not slept
or been awake. It's as if
I had sat all this time in the doorway
unable to move
and too dull to decide anything.
For the next hour there is still more light
here than inside, even if the lamp were lit.
I'll finish my wine.

*

When it began, I set a pail outside.
I threw off my clothes and washed
with soap and a tin cup. I could feel
the earth turning mud
under my feet. I liked it at first.
Now only snakes are drawn by the rain.
I almost stepped barefoot
on one this morning, a green-
yellow thing; it was just by the door.

*

I've no fire in the stove: yesterday
I forgot to fetch wood,
I was sulking; today it still rains.
One night I remember thinking
if all the stars fell, they could not fill
the cup I drank from. I feel
a kind of shame about this. Now I can't think
what it was made me happy; my emotions
seem little more than the weather.

The Tractor

The tractor has been junked for years.
Where it lies at the far end of the field
no one sees fit
to haul it away, and it has fixed
itself to the land, secure
as the mountains behind. At dusk

it becomes only a red blotch in that distance,
the last thing gone.
I have watched this happening
for the past hour or so from the fence;
on the other side a girl
is moving toward some horses

with a bridle, making small gestures at them.
She did not know whose tractor it was,
not her father's. South of us,
in the marshland, insects
and birds and frogs waken with the dark;
it is why she pointed

that way as she left, hearing them before me.
Louder now, their noise reaches
even into the houses. It is the sound
of an old machine
wheeling past us, impossible
to tell toward which direction or where it came from.

THE PAST IS A PLACE

New Poems

Burning Days, Luminous Sky

Burning days, luminous sky at dusk.
Stillness in the full water-pitcher on my desk,
stillness in the filled drinking glass and
in the slick telephone, its plug pulled from the wall.
At dusk I am thinking of the park again, I am there
in the shadow of a blue pine tree
while below, lights twinkle on and the city
hums under a starry silence far away
and an old dog dips her nose deeper into the grass.
Here is the safe place a happy man will come to
saying *This is not a mirage* — lips to the full glass.

The Old Streetcar Terminus, Parc Jean Cabot

I remember looking at condos near Parc Cabot
in the late eighties,
a park I'd known since early childhood
when mother took sister and me
to the Shriners Circus
opposite the streetcar terminus, at the Forum.
How strange our present
and past coexist
and never merge: the five-year-old
holding his circus toy,
a little fur monkey on a stick
later chewed to bits by the family dog,
the grave man with briefcase in hand
appearing in some condo doorway
or walking into a classroom
one block west of Parc Cabot, fifty years away,
to address students mostly sleeping.
Did the boy age
or was he put away some place
to lose substance as dreams do
when we join our waking life?
I can't say.
I just know he could be any small child
holding to his mother's coat sleeve at the circus,
not knowing the man he'd be one day.

The Pumpkin Field
    (Park Extension, 1957)
    for John Little

We are standing waist high in field weeds.
Moments ago the caboose man waved to us in his red car;
now the train, caterpillar size, vanishes
to the black bridge on the horizon.

We savour the caboose man's gesture.
That wave of the hand was a gift
sudden as the carnival that one morning camps
in the lot on Birnam Street and Howard
or the moment Bobby Nestruck's mother bends toward her son
and the long yellow braid appears.

In the train's wake we are watching the smoke plume,
the long black band
dissolving to air but now more real
than the vanished train.

We see the horizon is a ditch things fall into.
Never mind it. Today in the field weeds
we found a treasure of wild pumpkins — living,
rich, pulpy things.
In happiness little Bobby Nestruck pulls
one up and holds it in his arms.

On Salisbury Beach
>(An amusement park in the 1960s)
>*for Norm Sibum*

Showtime was dusk in the big cats' cage,
the first nightly performance on the midway,
and the cats were recalcitrant
in the spotlights' glare; massive, otherworldly
as Stonehenge megaliths,
they hunkered on their haunches
on their cramped perches and looked down
while concession lights above the midway
flashed violet and green in a darkening sky
and a summer night's crowd insistent as water
pressed the sideshow cage.

A thin mustached man who looked a stand-in
for Errol Flynn in some old late-night TV film,
some costume drama where musketeer chums
resemble disgruntled lions, this man
wore a frock-coat, trousers with a red stripe seam
and strangely in Massachusetts a pith helmet,
and he pulled the padlock
and from the chair by the door
picked up the whip: the whip snapped alive
in the light above his head, impressing the crowd,
not the sullen lion faces looking down.

Two men outside the cage shadowed the action,
one with a flame thrower, the other
a snub-nosed revolver. In the cage the whip cracked,
the trainer barked, the cats jumped.
They landed on soft cushion paws, climbed a ladder
Indian file like schoolchildren,

catwalked a long metal bar. Indifferent
to tightrope tricks, to show business, to applause,
four cats leapt back to their perches
and one for no reason fell upon the trainer,
pinned his shoulders to the floor — and
an electric current went humming through the crowd.

The trainer's death was unaccompanied
by fairground music or a barker's spiel;
the lion rolled aside like a big toy cat
with bullet holes in the head. I saw four other cats
on their high perches, cowed and forlorn, watching
and held back by a wing of yellow flame,
by the cries of handlers with wooden poles.

*

I saw what I shouldn't have seen, that evening.
I should have hidden my eyes
behind cotton candy when the moment came;
I should have gone to Witch Castle on Salisbury Beach;
I should have ridden The Whirlpool
or The Flying Horses to escape the cat-smelling cage.
Up there you can see the black Atlantic
only yards away; when the horses stop you hear the waves
grinding the shore, cold and removed
from Salisbury Park.

Caesar's Campaigns in Gaul
(Collège Notre Dame, 1963-64)

The Brothers of the Holy Cross:
I froze an ear one time shoveling their rink.
I could feel the numbness
as we filed up the stairs to morning classes.
Later, in the latrine mirror
I saw a boy in school blazer and tie, with a red
ear pointing at an angle.

One Friday I found my missing gym shirt
submerged in the communal drinking fountain;
this was my friend Labinne's humour.
I stuffed the shirt in my satchel
next to Caesar's *Campaigns in Gaul*.

Frère Crête remembered in Latin period
the Depression hoboes who came
to his parents' farm to beg a meal.
Once he brought us down to the music room,
took a fiddle from its black case, nestled
his chin and played.
He beat his toe to reels. Grey Frère Crête,
Skelette to us, was Lafontaine's grasshopper
come to life in a black soutane.

I wasn't angry about the ear.
I liked the rink and the blades'
chopping sounds as skaters
stepped from the change room.
Fridays, late afternoon, I skated alone
under grey metal cones strung along a wire.
I stood still in a grey light reflected from scraped ice.
Silence came in a wave of cold
washing into my lungs. Everyone had gone.

In the dark outside the rink
I wondered how the school's walls had swallowed
the footfalls and voices of my friends
who climbed stairs in rank and filed
down hallways in rank.
I saw not a trace of them there
nor in the serious or blank grad-picture faces
hanging on games-room walls,
nor in the pictures of boys who died in school
and never entered the world.

From the dorm window on a winter night,
I watched the snow fly into the darkness
across Queen Mary Road to the snow-shrouded steps
of L'Oratoire Saint-Joseph, and I remembered
the fall days when solitary pilgrims
climbed those steps on their knees.
Tier upon tier I followed their ascent.

Rooms to Let in Bohemia

Through the winter months, the last months I shared
with family, I was swayed by the spell of old places:
old houses with gingerbread on Prince Arthur;
the Milton Street laundry's sign, white board
with Chinese lettering over the door; Pine's
Duckpin Lanes above the pizzeria at Park and Pine
by the underpass; from the 80 bus window
I could see the bowlers slide and throw
as I headed south, into the past.

I remember the students of that distant time
as a tide of ghosts flooding McGill's grounds
and the McGill ghetto streets; the tide rushed past me,
and whatever thing the students dreamt
of reaching, they would reach fast, while my dream
happened two blocks down
in slow motion.
                        The Penelope, long gone,
was a haunt for blues and folk; flat-broke students
were left out on ice-grey pavement
stamping their numb feet before a marquee
without neon or flash — it said: Butterfield Blues
Tonight, Tim Hardin Next Week.
                           I looked three floors up
at a To Let sign wedged in a dormer window
in a row of windows. I looked at red brick
and the evening's snow
falling through winding fire escapes,
falling from floor to floor
through the iron grille,
and the window glowed down
in the drifting snow
like a magic lantern projecting a life
I could occupy: a room with a ceiling bulb
and a string.

                    I pulled the string
and the light went off and went
on in this life
I'd found three floors up from Bohemia
on Sherbrooke and Aylmer; elated
and solitary,
unable to afford a ticket,
I swayed to the music
of Butterfield, the music of Hardin.

The Afterlife

When I found one morning in June a room on Prince Arthur,
my parents looked forlorn and aged,
and they tried to surmount the long silence between us
and coax me to stay. Could I explain
my choosing to live in a room over a dark alley?
No one expected me to.
From me they expected whims, capricious choices.

My first meal from the Chinese grocer's on Park
was tinned water chestnuts.
I sat with my unopened can on the rooming-house steps;
funk music's groans swallowed the air round me, grinding
out the window of the downstairs room, the drug-parlour
    exchange
where business went on day and nightlong
to James Brown tunes, *Sex Machine*, *Hot Pants*.

Now the upstairs girl drifted down to the porch.
A scarecrow-thin girl who stuck needles
in her buttocks in her doorway across the hall,
she stood one step above me, a girl barely there
in black shirt and pants and scarecrow hat.
In disjointed steps she crossed the street,
seemed to float down the block.

She was someone living an afterlife
on Prince Arthur at the beginning of summer.
I saw her and didn't see.
At twenty I believed what I was seeing wasn't my life —
my life had yet to arrive — while the waif
across the hall knew hers was over.

I remember her one time on the front porch steps.
Between her thumb and index there's a wand
tipped in a ring. She dips it
in a soapy glass, twists
and lifts it to blow into the ring,
and iridescence rises out of her hand —
translucent spheres, luminous eggs.
She watches dead-still their ascent in the summer light.

Another time I remember
paramedics climbing the hot airless stairs.
They stand with their gear under the hall light,
wait for the janitor though the door is ajar.
Funk music from below grinds out the same tunes.
They pull on latex gloves before touching the body.

Tabagie Arsenault, 1920–1972

Arsenault's *Tobacco Magazines Novelties* is closing:
everyone has locked arms and is dancing.
The Arsenaults have given away flags, trinkets,
greeting cards from the '40s. Everyone dances
so that the floor shakes like the floor of a boat
while musicians huddle in a corner,
hardly noticing the audience,
and young men shouldering film cameras
as they circle the dancers
record for reasons known to film students
a rum bottle changing hands,
the singer's face, the girl next to me,
her blue eyelids and fingernails —
and there's a small dog here unseen by the cameras;
as the floor shakes, as the floor rolls, he jumps
straight up and barks at the noise everywhere.

Borrowed Days on Ste-Famille Street
   (March 1973)

Friday afternoon I hand Mme Bellefeuille
thirteen dollars' rent;
she opens her linen cabinet, drops
on my extended arms folded white sheets.
Here is the pleasure of a week's reprieve:
to walk up the stairs, sit
on the bedside holding fresh sheets.
Outside the March thaw cracks
and falls from shed roof to alley.
Voices — Beulah's telephone voice —
lilt and flutter
in the rooming-house walls, and Trépanier
again rearranges pots in his
allotted kitchen space. Here is the break and flow
of strange musical notes, strangers' lives
that vanish in a week or an hour on the day
rent is paid.

Almost one year away from my parents' home,
I survey my estate: hot plate, sink, some books
and this knowledge of time catching up
in the pause between afternoon and darkness.
What does a year leave?
I remember the burnt shreds of fireworks
on the street New Year's morning, burn smell
in the snow. I remember
an evening in August,
a stranger passing below in the alley,
the clacking of shoes moving toward me and away
without pause.

Now, years later, comes this surprise:

I've returned to Ste-Famille
looking for an address, an entrance, an access
to the rooming-house walls I remember —
if I could hear Beulah's voice
or have any proof the past is a place
not imaginary, a place —

I stand at the door, knock on it.

The Jacques Cartier Monument in Parc St-Henri

Once I thought of living on the park
to follow round the low iron fence
the passage of days
and know the fountain and know the circular path
beloved of dogs, walkers
and solitary sitters on a bench, but the park
faded as familiar things fade.

Now I can't remember the day
the clear falling water in the fountain stopped.
Was it the day after Thanksgiving? after All Saints?
Here my friend Carolyn sat between classes
as our students walked past.
The teachers, the park, the St. Henri metro
were way stations to them
as they passed into — who can say?
My friend died, the school moved away.
A vacant shell is left on St-Antoine
across from the factory, Imperial's sweet tobacco smell.

I remember the working years spent in that shell:
unreal, frittered away like days
in the abandoned movie theatres of my youth —
The Empire, The System, The Seville.
Though the show is long over,
slivers of light
slip through the cracks in the boarded doors;
a projectionist's light, it lingers
in the still, enclosed air
and does not illumine the past.
I turn to Jacques Cartier of St. Malo
standing poised above a dry fountain bed —

overhead, seagulls are circling
beyond his watch. Like a crossing guard
with one arm raised
in a ceaseless stopping motion,
he faces a schoolyard now deserted in St-Henri.

Carolyn's Pillbox Hat

Then came the reception out of town by a lake:
a January midday like grey March
friends family greeting and clasping
in a strange room and my friend's ashes
opposite the canapé table, a grey urn
polished and small
amid the cards, the good wishes

Outside across the road, fishermen are on the lake
tiny figures are bending to the ice
I want to turn to Carolyn now, touch her hand
say something about the weather
and the men maybe falling in

By this time her ghost is out the door,
she is wearing the leopard-skin hat
she wore the summer of her divorce,
the hat I admired over lunch twenty years ago,
a hat that said "F.O." to her ex, her two-timer ex

Now she is crossing Lambert Closse and de Maisonneuve,
her divorce behind her, a red-headed woman
and a pillbox hat, and a wave
and a wave of the hand — the hat set
just so to the left

A Cowhide Mitten Made in China

I was a bird owner in '84. One November evening
I came home knowing I would find him dead,
and he was dead, stiff toppled on his side
in the gravel

Then I remembered not the songs
but the pain of the last years: his red claws
twisted and scaled with arthritis
could not hold the bars,

he coughed in the dirt, made strange
clicking sounds down there alone
He was an old bird, ten years old in '84

I took my friend and slipped
him in a cowhide mitten made in China
I brought him across Marlowe to the railroad tracks,
dug a hole and that

was that, except
when an innocent thing leaves the world
it seems to leave in pieces: the songs

flutter, pull your insides and come back —
songs relentless, insane even
like a bird panicking at a window to get out,
knocking itself cold at last

It's not a thing you forget in an evening
though I tried
I took the cage, gravel, seed and
my friend in his leather coffin

and threw them away,
I mean
I threw them from my heart

Otis, how could death treat you so rudely
to collect only a small thing, small
feathers, finally nothing
on the scale?

Twenty years past, I remember still
the day your wings clicked and beat
up and down the kitchen
door glass, a winter sky beyond.

Coming Home to a Flat Where a Light Is Left On
    (East Verdun, 1974)

Dusk comes early in December;
winter dampness sinks
like a cold breath in the chest.
Now the black ice on Evelyn Street shines
and streetlamps dim
in the distance of a city block
growing longer at dusk,
now the iron staircases of old triplexes
from Regina to Hickson
waver as they rise,
balconies deserted but one:
there an inflated Santa Claus
in a sleigh in a ring of white lights
is waving from a neighbour's second story
and I think, *Nothing changes in Verdun.*
I put my key in the door — open it
and a wave of cold rushes past.

    *

Dusk came early the day they entered my flat.
(A neighbour said, The Regina Street Gang;
I knew then it was a cover for his friends.)
You learn the poor robbing the poor is nothing new.
They'll take old records, they'll take
a lame typewriter with a broken carriage bar
and a scratched pocket watch made in Ukraine ...
The kitchen window is kicked open,
a yellow bird cringes on the floor of his cage
in a draft that jars you
where you stand in the hall of your railroad flat,
staring at the light left on.

From the back steps you walk to the fence
and look into the darkness of the lane.
What could they have taken
that leaves a sinking emptiness?
Tonight you picture your neighbour's friends,
you picture one
like Santa Claus with a sack on his back
hitting the flats, jumping
the back fences of east Verdun,
and as he advances the sack is leaking crumbs,
you see it leaking its strange abundance,
the crumbs of your life.

On the Winter Steps

On the winter steps of Alexis Nihon,
a nameless man in a grey coat lies on his side.
One hand crooked under his cheek,
he stares down the Plaza's
concrete steps, blue eyes vacant, set,
as shoppers sidestep his still form at the door
and move inside. Corpse and climbers
ignore each other. He stares bereft and unwelcome,
they stay the course, keeping the apparition
out of their sight and their balance
in check. *You!* I say,
and move on, wondering
what consolation we can offer the dead.
Money, art, love — they won't accept it.
On the winter steps of Alexis Nihon,
the dead are greeted like poor relations.

A Late Night Walk

Why does the old dog
struggle from her blanket
and on shaky legs cross the floor
to look up into my face?

                         Hers
is the fixed, startled
look of old age,
it is the hand a beggar thrusts at you
at the subway door,
it is a stone
planted in the wastes of your heart

                      How many
nights have we walked together
this street, failing the same question
pulling at the leash?
I don't know

                      The poem
of time I was meant to write
has not died a peaceful death

The Dalai Lama at St. Joseph's Oratory

My neighbour, whom I dislike,
is still yacking
though the Dalai Lama has risen to address us
He speaks at the basilica's head,

holding with one hand his yellow and maroon robe;
I like the little authoritative, academic gesture
that signals his interpreter
he's finished a segment of his speech

Now thousands stand ecstatic on their seats,
rain applause on the fourteenth incarnation
of the Buddha of Compassion
There'll be raves in tomorrow's papers,

but why, moments ago,
did I burst into tears
while the procession slowly moved up the nave of St. Joseph's?

I have a twentieth century show-biz appreciation
of pageantry, and anyway
the tears I wept were not tears of joy

In the floodlights I see
a single human face
making a plea for brotherhood

and later, when holy men of various faiths
exchange white silk scarves with Dalai Lama
I see one Indian, Mohawk or Cree, in a red beaded shirt
present him an eagle's feather

They look at each other — Oh I know everything here
including the feather
is staged — but when they look at each other
I see the vanquished peoples of America greeting

vanquished Tibetans, I see
a trail of corpses and their ghosts
come to haunt us a little longer and leave

So they greet each other, fingers touching the feather
Brothers meeting strangely
in a white man's gargantuan basilica, they can smile
while thousands cheer and howl on their seats

And I am weeping again, I am
the one, the modern man, descendant of victors,
who in a lifetime received from strangers
this one glimpse of brotherhood

Six Months After

Six months after the heart attack
Aunt Dot still has her cats, and the tree
planted in '86 — the year of mother's
cancer diagnosis — the apple tree
in the small dirt yard in Verdun,
has grown tall enough to fit a bench under.

My mother and aunt sit there now, holding hands.
As girls they were best friends and loved to hide
down the hall in the deacon's bench
where Nana kept the scarves and winter things.
Hide and seek, sixty-five years ago.

The old women sit under a backyard tree
on a June evening. White cats
lie on the porch steps and windowsill,
a baseball broadcast drifts through the screen.
They are silent, each knowing the place.

Somewhere there is a photograph
of two little girls on a country road — sisters
by their eyes' expression, haircuts and rough-made dresses.
The taller one has just touched the other's shoulder;
she is squinting into the camera lens,
peering down the road.

A Soldier's End on de L'Epée Street

I heard he died alone that afternoon
without morphine, without family.
I wanted to solace his unloved ghost
and wondered if my wishes traveled the distance,
and if ghosts had ears did they maybe
not want to hear from us in their wake.

My uncle had known long journeys in the dark,
had driven troops on night roads across Europe's war
and when he came home in '45 he burned his uniform
on the balcony over the alley on de L'Epée, his wife
and young son watching in the kitchen door.

He drove a truck for Eaton delivery
then an MTC streetcar, then a bus.
He rose in the four a.m. dark for his route
down Côte des Neiges skirting the cemetery,
a green distance he hoped one day to lie in.

At the end Uncle Bert could not lie or sit;
he was dying of his kidneys
and refused hospital, dialysis, all of it.
He faced death alone on the hall floor,
his wife gone out to her shopping.
Returning, with my mother, Aunt Margaret shoved
at the weight against the door — at Uncle Bert,

whose last journey on earth
was his tortoise crawl to the front door.
The two women, my aunt and my mother,
stood with brown grocery bags in their arms
in the dim light of a January afternoon.
Mother stared down at Uncle Bert, as the years
closed and her own death wedged against her chest.

The Art of Departure

1   When Aunt Doris Learned Alzheimer's Had Taken Her Sister

The old women, the contraband shoppers,
at the bus stop in Plattsburgh, in the minutes
before the bus to Montreal arrived,
were hiding parcels and snipping tags off clothes
they would slink over the border.
They were lighthearted, they sounded
like children on an outing.
Doris saw her sister, my mother, step
off the curb into the oncoming traffic.
Standing in the wind and blare of passing cars,
mother was not afraid.
She was like a small willful child
climbing stairs one by one; she didn't look back.
Somewhere ahead, through the speeding car lanes,
was her life — her old life,
before the weight of loss made her heart cave,
made her wander nights from room to room,
weep or fall silent on the phone while Doris
read from a book of prayers. Was there a prayer
for this occasion? Now she wailed *Connie,
Connie!* after my mother, who did not look or flinch.
Encumbered with parcels Doris ran into the street.

2   What Aunt Margaret Said to My Mother a Year Earlier

Under the weight of a failing heart
Margaret wavered in the street; her shoulders sagged,
her legs sagged, her wind was vapour in her mouth.
Standing at the curb on Howard, mother looked
and said, "I'll stay with you, we'll go home."
Margaret shrugged, refused her sister as she refused hospital:
"I'll get used to it," she said — the words
she spoke the day her husband died — and Margaret
died alone that night
collapsed on the bedside with her beads in her hands.
She was ready as her mother had been: grandmother,
Elizabeth, who ignored the daughter at her hospital bedside
and spoke these last words,
"I was happy to live, I'm happy to die."
Nana was a poor charwoman, another tough saint
with no use for goodbye; no matter
the ties of love or blood, in the end
she would turn her head, leave family at the curbside.

A Prelude

The plot was on a rise;
we had to climb to it, stand lopsided
at the graveside while rain fell
on December snow, on the ground at our feet
like a prelude to the new year's storm.

The family of stragglers was about to leave
when the old woman's youngest son, my cousin,
insisted on shaking everyone's hand
and showily hugged his older brother,
who appeared this morning
after twenty years, jetlagged
and jettisoned in a back pew of St. Francis.

As I entered the church, the younger brother
turned in his seat: I saw a thin face, a goatee,
a removed look. I searched for the boy's face
in the man's and as I looked
the priest began the funeral mass
though he was dying on his feet.

His eulogy remembered Margaret's devotions
at the Stations of the Cross
and her dusting the church statuary,
St. Francis and St. Roch,
but the family knew Margaret in her last year
had got confused, would bang daily
on the rectory door, demanding Sunday mass.
For Margaret, every day had become Sunday.

And the priest, Father Kirouac,
whose most constant parishioner
was demented — I wonder,

did he open the door to her?
Was there patience in his face
as he knew, more or less,
they would both be gone before spring?

After mass, seated on the altar steps,
he apologized in shallow breaths
for not accompanying us to the grave.
He outlived her by six weeks.

Borrowed Minutes, Dying in Hospital

On the Cardiac-and-Respiratory floor
your loved one's body
suddenly turns inert bric-a-brac
now small on the hospital bed,
and Code Blue's bells and siren wail
(you checked *Code* on the form) make dying
twisted theatre for you, but not staff.
For staff, dying is business
and nothing personal.

A legion of attendants hustles down the floor.
Wheeling trolley, carting paddles
& black bag and hypo in fist they plug in
and throw you out. It's nothing personal.
The respiratory technician by reception
repeats the patient was breathing
after she suctioned her. *Breathing.*
A word, a talisman. It resounds down the floor,
hollow to you. Business to them.

Suctioning's rasping sound drove me from the room.
Round midnight I was one floor below
in a deserted canteen, then drifted to cardio
then waited down the hall for the technician to leave
then found she was gone and the room empty
except for my mother's body now still
and no longer gasping air,
and the phone rang.
Call it telepathy. Who knows.

In the hall by reception they watch and say nothing.
An infinity of minutes weighs in the chest.
You sit on a hard chair
and survive in instants. Down the floor
a door opens, a tall man with erect posture approaches;
his smile meant to reassure next-of-kin
reassures you. You trust him
and yet you don't. He's
chief of resuscitation, he's business.

He says after thirty minutes the vital signs
are machine induced, nothing more,
we're prolonging her death. You wonder how often
he's said *prolonging death* to get consent
to disconnect — and he smiles once more.
Someone, a nurse, places a hand on your shoulder
and a wave passes over you; it feels
not like death but all of life passing over you
as you sit on a hard chair in the hall by reception.

Soon family will arrive and staff will remove the body.
I'm alone now with my mother.
I see under a thin sheet a child's corpse of seventy pounds,
stripped of ring, clothes and crucifix.
I see her dentures in a small cup and beside it
a silver-coloured angel, a Christmas ornament.
Her jaw is slack, her hair stiff.
I've shut her eyelids;
I'm scraped of every human feeling except shame.

*

Once I remember she wanted me to be attentive,
to listen in school. I wonder, what is there
now to be attentive to? I'm remembering

an evening in August '76. Mother has just
seen her first grandchild in Maternity;
we're waiting at the bus stop on Park Avenue
for the number 80 north to take her home.
Here it turns round the corner. Soon
it will go through the Pine underpass,
soon the bandstand and angel monument
across Fletcher's Field
will appear in the passenger's window.
A solitary woman is traveling at night
and as the landmarks pass by her
they are more felt than seen;
this I know as her little journey
continues in me now, continues stop by stop.

I see her climbing into the bus
slowly, fearful of falling; she leans forward,
deposits her coins in the coin box.
I'll call tomorrow, I say, meaning *love*
and *be safe*. She turns
and is already in another world.
The door is closed, the bus pulls away.

The Sea beyond the Coast of Maine

I   My Father's Things

Today I found a Lieutenant Governor's medal
on a shelf in a box of my father's things,
the odd things I haven't thrown away.
The grey medal rested in my hand and time
flipped back: it was his last stay in hospital,
it was the day he died quietly
after breakfast when the nurse was on her break
and the woman sharing the semi-private
didn't notice her roommate was dead.

How he needed the world's notice! The need
filled my parents' apartment, a storage
apartment, a shed and garage
with trophies, ribbons, plaques — detritus
of bowling, beekeeping and show-dog competitions —
with CV's and boxes of business cards
boosting his company, *Clé Succès*.

In the end the need left my poor father
to drown and sink, frightened and unprotesting,
causing not even a ripple.
When the hospital called, the voice
in my ear held back the news
as if I had to guess, and when it came to the subject
it snickered and faltered. Later in the room
I kissed his face and felt a rigid absence,
and a shadow slipped past me and disappeared.

2   At Sea

Back then, in lifetimes that seem far as stars
beyond reach, what were we?
Not friends, not enemies,
only father and son and it meant
not much or it meant
nearly everything; in the last count
it meant we were in the same boat.

So, that noon,
we set out in our small boat,
pulling oars and sliding out of port
along the coast of Maine,
and we held in our sight
a long black bridge,
landmark to secure the return home.

In a small boat
you sit almost down in the water;
you sit, man and boy, in a close space.
The weather then is seized in the salt air,
in the clouds' amoeba growth overhead,
in the winds' sweep and your boat's sway
and bump over the sea waves.

And the bridge
fades into a pencil scratch
in the grey distance.
You look at your father bent over his fishing line
grim and absorbed
in some remote adult interest, and guess
you'd rather drown here than ask to go home.

The fishing line
tough as clothesline slips
through your fists hand-over-hand
into the green sea now calm. You sit
with the clam-bait smell sticking to your shirt
and pants, and the fish
come up: flat fish, sad gasping creatures
curling in spasm on the boat floor.

Under the plank seat
the fish linger on; you wonder how much longer,
you wonder aloud, for no reason,
"How much do fishermen make by the hour?"
Now your father's voice
is harsh, incensed, "I'm not paying
you to fish!" and the boat shakes — it shakes
in fits sudden and hard to throw us in the deep.

Misunderstandings
are not discussed or forgotten; we grip
the oarlocks and wait. The day is over
but for this: from the dark water
a disklike shadow rises and settles under the boat.
It is large and sinuous. It undulates
its fins slowly, luxuriantly, sways
and glides unconcerned away from us.

And the millstone
of silence still weighs in the boat.
If I could speak to him now
as I never did then, surely I would say

what everyone says: *Does it matter
what we fought over?
Where, father, have our lives gone?*

And he would say —

    He would say —

3   The Distance

In the late afternoon, in the failing light
off the coast of Maine, my father
is rowing home toward the bridge,
has been rowing hard for hours —
how I wish I were with him! — but the bridge
remains as is, a pencil scratch
in the distance,
and the distance never changes.

Clover, Buckwheat, Wildflower Honey

Father said nothing about it.
Mother said he kept the hives in a clover field
somewhere north of the city.
Trèfle, Sarrasin, Fleurs sauvages fin d'été:
I see his script on adhesive strips,
labels stuck to tins and jars of pale amber wildflower
and clover and dark gold buckwheat.

A Saturday morning, late September,
his station wagon points out of the driveway.
He wears a camel-tan sport coat, his frame bends
to arrange honey tins on the car floor.
His greying hair, his closed
preoccupied face give nothing away.
Rolled-up sheets of paper, notes on his day's schedule,
poke out of his sport coat pocket.

From the parlour window I would spy on my father,
a man who longed to be away,
and though I never longed to be near him
as the car pulled away, I wondered,
felt uneasy as I knew, standing there
holding the drape folds,
that something was passing; I wondered
why such secrecy was needed to sell honey at market
Saturday morning, why the need suffused everything he did.

Come end of summer, some other year,
the driveway's blacktop
is covered with reddish-brown husks of dead bees,

the station wagon is junk somewhere
and my father, who believed the progress of science
would unlock mysteries,
my father, exactly who he was, is now a secret
as good as locked in a shell of compacted steel,
a secret passed beyond science's reach and mine.

The Shoes of Budapest
"To the memory of the victims shot into the Danube by Arrow Cross militiamen ..." — INSCRIPTION ON A HOLOCAUST MEMORIAL PLAQUE IN BUDAPEST.

Some photos are hard to take: this one, for instance,
of a row of shoes twenty paces long, old brown shoes
dwarfed by miles of grey riverbank,
an odd memorial to the shoeless
in the Danube — no one knows how many.

For now we've got 120 cast-iron shoes cemented to
　　the riverbank
so no souvenir fanatic can steal them,
no aesthete can rearrange them
and no skinhead can kick them into the Danube.

The shoes are sculptured to look worn,
almost human, like shoes in a painting by van Gogh.
Mourners have left candle stubs and flowers
in some of them to remember
the numberless, the barefoot on the river floor.

Life Jacket Drill on a Ship Off San Juan
(In Memoriam: Hart Crane)

At dusk, on deck, in a line of passengers
a thousand long, I think of Hart Crane as he fell
from the Orizaba's stern into the sea,
and the sea's current north of Havana
drew him down.

Now the young crewman — *Emergency Guide*
printed on his shirt —
moves us through the drill.
He slips over his head the orange jacket,
blows a hollow breath into the whistle, touches

the signal light; then, holding the jacket
like a dance partner, he mimes a quick two-step,
a brief delight for passengers numb
to the possibility of drowning, bored dead
on their feet.

Beyond the ship, dusk leeches the sea of green.
The sea at dusk turns a repository of black cloud,
a rapture of memory; melancholic,
iridescent,
it flashes and shifts like the skin
of a sea creature or a mirror of the heart,

and I think of Hart Crane, poet laureate of the sea,
as his lover remembered him
in an old black-and-white film,
the morning he came into the cabin and sat on the bed:
"Everything is lost, I've got to go."
And Peggy Cowley laughed, said stay on for breakfast.

Hart by this time knew his craft had left him.
A poem now was a soured lover, a dance partner
that wouldn't dance,
and he didn't want a life jacket
to free-fall into delirium or a long blackout
of boredom.

Remembering that morning, Peggy had an inward look:
"They brought in a menu to him
and I don't think he left one item out —
just an enormous meal —
he wanted to be filled with something."
And he left her then, plummeted one step
into the green void above the sea.

"The boat had been stopped
and bells were ringing;
they were letting down the first boats to look for him."
In the last picture frame, surprise — discovery —
was the look in Peggy's face, her eyes:
an old woman, a young girl remembering
Hart Crane had once been alive like you or me.

In the Hills of St. Lucia

In the hills of St. Lucia, in the rain forest
the black poison tree is a leafless
massive trunk; coarse, secretive,
recessed in shadow it rises
to a vanishing point, a tree without limbs.

Tourists, we gaze into the woods' deep ceiling,
into the spill of rain
that wets faces, gums clothes to skin
while the path softens underfoot
and our tour guide, disdaining rain,
resumes his set piece on the local banana crop,
on coconut linen, the hibiscus flower
and parasite-fungus growth,
which some fallen thing by the path
now wears like a soft dark glove.

As for the tree, "Even a speck,"
the guide's tone drops to a whisper,
"even a molecule
of the black root or bark
will kill neighbours, competitors, in-laws..."
He mimics a shiver and moves on,

leaving us exposed — cold and sad-faced
as stray dogs in a downpour,
gazing up at the black tree of fairy tales,
which is poisonous
and indifferent to designs
of the human heart.

Stray Dogs of St. Lucia

1

Rodney Bay, the tour's last stop,
is white stucco beach-hotels
and three stray dogs under a jagged palm.
Aware of us and strangely aloof,
they waver on the periphery of our vision,
meander toward us with the slowness of hunger,
creatures we see
as flotsam with dogs' ears, a blot
on the ocean's shore.

One comes near: red-rimmed eyes
in a fleshless skull,
a non-committal look
and a mouth that gently pulls
fried plantains from my fingers,
lets slivers fall in the dirt...
With her ribs jutting out,
her pregnant belly jutting out
and her spine's ridges
like a salamander curving under the skin,
she lives on on Rodney Bay,
strange survivor, life force
that humbles me — a life force I revere.

2

In her last year on Wiseman Avenue,
my mother's second childhood, her illness,
marooned her, left her locked in a dark hallway
repeating odd sounds, ravaged phrases,
mother and *home* the only words I remember ...

Once, long before the Alzheimer's set in,
mother installed above her Roxton colonial sofa
a print of Renoir's *Déjeuner des Canotiers*.
On an island in the Seine young Parisians
in boater hats lounge in modish decorum
and drink under a rose canopy in the midday light.
A seated girl in the left foreground
leans slightly forward, oblivious to her companions
as she closes her eyes with pleasure.
Under a straw hat pinned with pink flowers,
she murmurs endearments to a grey wisp, a dog
that is like a feather duster with bangs.
She holds the dog firmly in her hands and whispers.
The dog leans to her, pressing his paws
against her white collar, and looks up,
a bit puzzled. The eyes glow with attention.

3

Three mongrel dogs lie in the sun, their legs
stretched to the sea …
Mother, who loved dogs, said once
that old age turns us into strays.
I don't remember my answer, yet today
someone, a stray at life's edge,
has come and gone and knows me,
has greeted me and gone — strange survivor,
life force I bow to, here on Rodney Bay.

Late Recognition
(A poetry reading at Dawson College)
for Louis Dudek

"Hello, Professor!"
That made Louis turn in his seat.
"You can't possibly recognize me," he said
and turned again; still I knew
his serious look,
the listening posture
as he sat straight on a fold-up chair,
an old poet with a cane across his lap
and a tweed cap in a bony fist.

He hemmed, hawed, pushed out his lower lip,
waited to hear a true poem, a godsend,
or at least a true line
a poet might craft from his notes,
while the lineup of poets reading on stage
fell short one by one.

Louis Dudek now held a closed hand up to my face;
his tone was magisterial and slightly amused:
"Who can tell if this handful of dust
had once been a mule or a man?"
He named an ancient Greek poet, the fist
turned over and spread,
and I looked into empty space
for the dust of a human life falling from his hand.

On a spring afternoon of his retirement
he came to hear the young ones read.
While they postured he waited
for the true poem that never appeared,
and no one knew him:

they saw another old man with a cap and a cane,
a fold-up life, a fold-up chair.

Louis thought none of this unfair or strange.
Once he told me it was time I recognized
the fate of most literary men
is anonymity — has always been;
he said (he was pleased with the phrase)
Their bones litter the bottom of the sea.

A Fall

Unprepared for it, you fall —
hear yourself crack — into old age.
You can lie still or crawl away
like some roadkill only half-killed
or shift like a bundle of clothes
tossed on the dark boulevard,
but you can't get up — or out.
Pavement potholes wait for the next
pedestrian, driver, fool
while you await your life's next stage
as if knocking at the door
of a club whose membership you'd avoid
given the choice. Choice?
You fall with a crack and can't get out.

Gospel Music in Little Burgundy

Saturday evening choir practice
at the Pentecostal church: over the chorus
the soloist's voice, a dark hook,
pitches across a deep marine sky
across rue Vinet, *O happy day, O happy day!*
and a spasm of voices rises, harmonizes
above the church, above the belfry
with the one small bell; voices
which tomorrow will sway enveloped
in white, orange and yellow surplices
rise higher *to watch and pray and rejoice*
and at the hymn's break — small moment
of stillness — piano chords rumble and echo
in a great empty hall,
and the soloist's voice like Mavis Staples'
drops lower, deeper, intones
almost with regret, *'Twas a happy day, a happy day*
and the chorus's response flares
When Jesus washed, when he washed my sins away!

Call and response angle and troll
through the summer air; the aural trance,
the hook, reaches into the ear
and tugs. The Pentecostal choir practises
at being fishers of men,
night fishing in Little Burgundy
while in the park below,
in the bushes adjoining the church,
dealers, hookers and johns
go on trading favours, pursuing business
beyond a fisherman's lure.

Greyhound to Burlington

It rains and stops the morning long; we sleep
the long drive through mountain clouds.
Tomorrow, who will remember this?
Mist floating like moss in the pine trees,
grey mist blurring the mountains to memory; now
blossoms peck and spatter the glass, the windshield
wipers not moving, not moving yet.

The Unitarian Churchyard in Burlington
"My own mind is my own church."
— THOMAS PAINE

In the shade of a berry tree I look
to the green and white steeple that pins
the August sky like a sheet
of paper, vast, cloudspecked, untroubled
by errors or human wrongs. Below,

a man plays with a scruffy mongrel:
the dog meanders till his master whistles,
then he runs. On Sunday
man and dog are happiest.

In the haze of late afternoon sun
the churchyard lawn is tinged with yellow, printed
with shadows of well-spaced trees
and the clock in the tower has long stopped.
Now a single bird flies through the tall steeple.

As Tom Paine, according to the sign-
board on the lawn, found his own church
in his own mind, so the bird finds
pleasure in its dark flight. And may the phantoms

in my own human mind
find rest today, Sunday, dear God; may the bird
vanish as it passes through the steeple, may the dark
wing be a shadow passing lightly
through the air of Tom Paine's church.

Notes

"Life Jacket Drill on a Ship Off San Juan": In 1931-32 Peggy Cowley and her husband, the literary critic Malcolm Cowley, were in the midst of a divorce when Peggy went to Mexico to establish residency; there she began a love affair with the poet Hart Crane. The film the poem alludes to — directed by Lawrence Pitkethly and co-written by Derek Walcott and Margot Feldman — belongs to a series of documentaries on American poets titled *Voices and Visions*. Peggy Cowley recounts Hart Crane's final moments in the last few minutes of the film. Their ship sailed out of Vera Cruz and was bound for New York.

"Late Recognition": When he spoke the words, "their bones litter the bottom of the sea," Louis Dudek may have been consciously or unconsciously invoking the ending of A. M. Klein's poem, "Portrait of the Poet as Landscape": *Meanwhile, he/ makes of his status as zero a rich garland,/ a halo of his anonymity,/ and lives alone, and in his secret shines/ like phosphorus. At the bottom of the sea.*" I wish I could speak to him about it because I am curious and because I miss him.

Acknowledgements

Earlier versions of these poems appeared in various print publications, were recorded on LP, and were broadcast on radio. I am grateful to the editors of *The Antigonish Review*, *The Canadian Forum*, *The Fiddlehead*, *Impulse*, *Intercourse*, *Lion's Head* (online), *Mainline*, *Miss Chatelaine*, *New American & Canadian Poetry*, *The New Quarterly*, *The Tamarack Review*, and *The Wascana Review*; the anthologies, *Cross/cut: Contemporary English Quebec Poetry*, *Four Montreal Poets*, *Ten Montreal Poets* at the CEGEPs (with accompanying recording), *The Penguin Book of Canadian Verse* (second revised edition), *The Speaking Earth*, and *Storm Warning*; the collections, *Touchings* (1970) and *The White Magnet* (1973); and to Robert Weaver of the CBC.

I wish to thank the Canada Council for the Arts for generous support in years past.

Finally, I would especially like to thank Robyn Sarah and Norm Sibum. Without their faith, encouragement and attention to my work, this book would not be. "Thank you" seems a grossly inadequate return for the generosity they showed me.

About the Author

Marc Plourde was born in Montreal in 1951 of French and English Canadian parents and has been writing and translating poetry for over forty years. A graduate of l'Université de Montréal, he has worked as a freelance literary translator and as a college English teacher. He has published collections of poetry and short stories as well as many translations, including Gaston Miron's selected poems, *Embers and Earth*, which he co-translated with the poet D. G. Jones.